# Tunes for Alto Saxophone Technic

## by Major Herman Vincent in collaboration with Fred Weber

## To The Teacher

One of the most effective and enjoyable ways to develop technical dexterity on an instrument is through melodies of a technical nature and with scale and rhythm variation based on familiar melodies. TUNES FOR TECHNIC is designed with this in mind. Because tunes, melodies and technical variations are interesting and more enjoyable to practice, most students will work more effectively, and over-all results will be excellent. Some of the melodies and variations in TUNES FOR TECHNIC may be challenging and difficult. In this case work up slowly and accurately, then gradually increase tempo. In general, the book progresses in difficulty and correlates with the method book, "The Alto Sax Student," Part I. It may be also used in conjunction with any elementary alto sax method.

The Belwin "STUDENT INSTRUMENTAL COURSE" - A course for individual and class instruction of LIKE instruments, at three levels, for all band instruments.

*EACH BOOK IS COMPLETE IN ITSELF BUT ALL BOOKS ARE CORRELATED WITH EACH OTHER*

**METHOD**

**"The Alto Saxophone Student"**

**For individual**

**or**

**class instruction.**

*ALTHOUGH EACH BOOK CAN BE USED SEPARATELY, IDEALLY, ALL SUPPLEMENTARY BOOKS SHOULD BE USED AS COMPANION BOOKS WITH THE METHOD*

**STUDIES AND MELODIOUS ETUDES**

Supplementary scales, warm-up and technical drills, musicianship studies and melody-like studies.

**TUNES FOR TECHNIC**

Technical type melodies, variations, and "famous passages" from musical literature — for the development of technical dexterity.

**THE ALTO SAXOPHONE SOLOIST**

Interesting and playable graded easy solo arrangements of famous and well-liked melodies. Also contains 2 Duets, and 1 Trio. Easy piano accompaniments.

**DUETS FOR STUDENTS**

Easy duet arrangements of familiar melodies for early ensemble experience.
Available for: Flute
Bb Clarinet
Alto Sax
Bb Cornet
Trombone

# Contents

# Old MacDonald

# Looby Lou

# Yankee Doodle

# Pop Goes The Weasel

B.I.C.133

# Peasant Dance

# A-Tiskit A-Taskit

# Pop Goes The Weasel

# Down In The Valley

Moderato

# Drink To Me Only With Thine Eyes

# Crusaders' Hymn

B.I.C.133

# Waltz Melody

NAGELI

# I Love You Truly

BOND

# Melody From Poet And Peasant Overture

VON SUPPE

# Sidewalks Of New York

LAWLOR – BLAKE

# Onward Christian Soldiers

A. SULLIVAN

Play in accented style

# The Victors

ELBEL

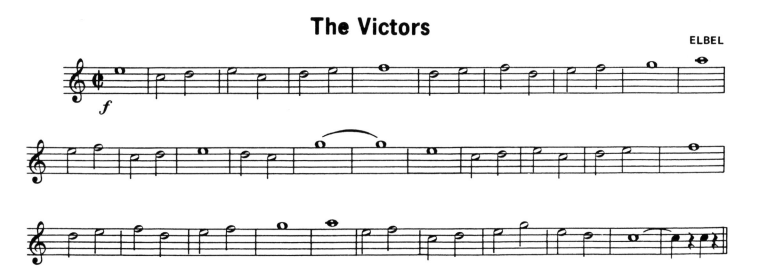

# The Band Played On

WARD

# Hungarian Dance Theme

BRAHMS

Count **4/4**    1   2   3   4

Count **¢**    1   +   2   +

# Theme From High School Cadets March

SOUSA

# Swanee River

FOSTER

*Fine*

*D. S. al Fine*

# Home, Sweet Home

BISHOP

# El Capitan Theme

SOUSA

like C♯

# Joyce's 71st Regiment March Theme

BOYER

# Sleeping Beauty Waltz

TSCHAIKOWSKY

Valse lento

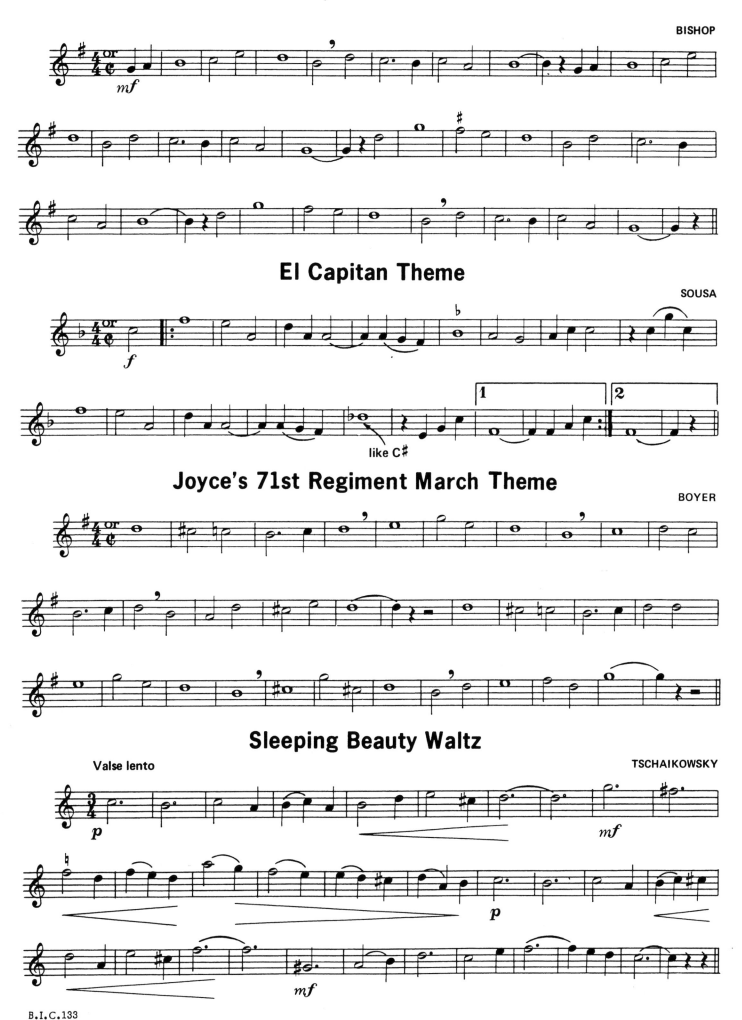

B.I.C.133

# Gold And Silver Waltz

LEHAR

# Rainbow Theme

CHOPIN

# S. I. B. A. March

HALL

## Sakura Sakura
*A Japaneese Folk Tune*

## You're A Grand Old Flag

COHAN

## Fiesta

BOREL – CLERE

## Long, Long Ago

## Long, Long Ago

## Russian Melody

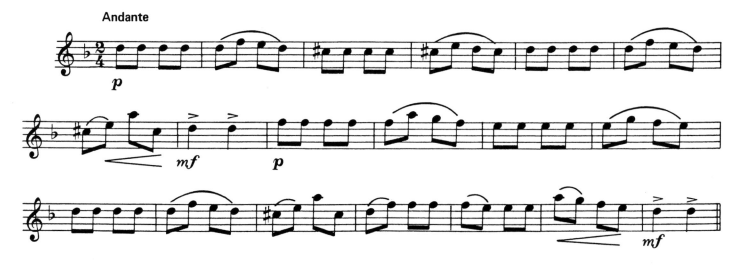

## English Melody

## Buffalo Gals

**Allegro**

## Up On The Housetop

**Allegro**

## We Wish You A Merry Christmas

## Loch Lamond

# The Blue Bells Of Scotland

Moderato

# Tambourin

ROMEAU

# John Peel

ENGLISH HUNTING SONG

# She'll Be Comin' Round The Mountain

# VARIATIONS ON A FAMOUS THEME

**Work this page out carefully, then try for speed.**

*Melody*

MOZART

## Rhythm Variation I In Key Of C

## Scale Variation I In Key Of C

# Roses From The South

J.STRAUSS

# Our Director

BIGELOW

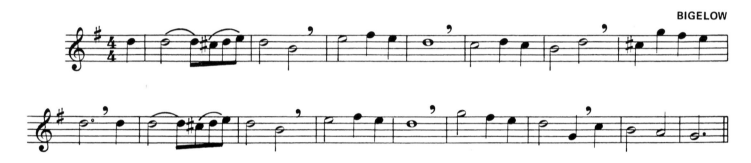

# The Dying Cowboy

# Cara Nome

VERDI

# THEME AND VARIATIONS

**Theme**

NURSERY RHYME

*Rhythm Variation In C*

*Rhythm Variation In D*

*Scale Variation In C*

*Scale Variation In D*

Octave key only

B.I.C.133

# Sharpshooter's March

METALO

# Father Of Victory March

GANNE

# The Violins Play

PAGANINI

*Fine*

*D.C. al Fine*

# TUNES AND VARIATIONS
## Polly Wolly Doodle

## Marines' March

# Auld Lang Syne

# Hymn Of Thanksgiving

# Adeste Fidelis

# VARIATION
## America The Beautiful

WARD

*Tonguing Fun*
**Moderato**

## Jewish Folk Song

## In The Gloaming

# Blow The Man Down

*Melody*

**Tonguing Variation In C**

# Melody In A

*A Tonguing Tune*

# Emperor Waltz

J. STRAUSS

## Melody By Borodin

BORODIN

## Santa Lucia

## Tschaikowsky Concerto Theme

TSCHAIKOWSKY

# Waltz Viennese

STRAUSS

# Skaters Waltz

WALTEUFEL

*Chordal Variation*

# Yippie Ti Yi Yo

# Sonatina

**Moderato**

BEETHOVEN

*Fine*

*D. C. al Fine*

# Largo

DVORAK

# Minuet

**Moderato — not too fast**

MOZART

*Fine*

*D. S. al Fine*

## Merry Widow Waltz

## Drink To Me Only With Thine Eyes

## Gold And Silver Waltz

Work out all Melodies on this page Carefully, then try for Speed with Accuracy.

# Song Of The Reapers

R. SCHUMAN

## Battle Hymn Of The Republic

## Long, Long Ago With Variations

*Melody*

*Variation I*

*Variation II*

Work out all Melodies on this page Carefully, then try for Speed with Accuracy.

# Carnival Of Venice

Slow - 6 beats per measure

Slowly

March tempo

*Scale Variation* Work out carefully, then try for speed.

Work out all Melodies on this page Carefully, then try for Speed with Accuracy.

# Theme From The Thunderer March

March tempo

SOUSA

# Dance Etude

Not too fast

STREABORG

*Fine*

*D.C. al Fine*

# Happy Dance

Andante

PURCELL

*mf*

# Greensleeves

Moderato — 6 beats per measure.

Work out all Melodies on this page Carefully, then try for Speed with Accuracy.

# Jingle Bells

*Melody*

*Scale Variation*

# Sailor's Hornpipe

Work out Carefully, then try for Speed with Accuracy.

Work out all Melodies on this page Carefully, then try for Speed with Accuracy.

## Variation On Yankee Doodle

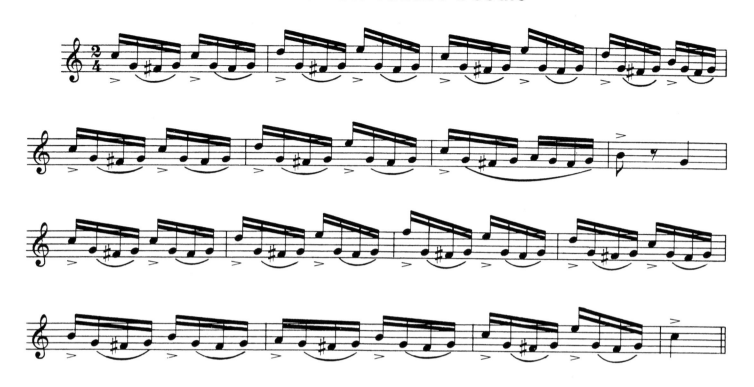

## March By Mozart

MOZART

Work out all Melodies on this page Carefully, then try for Speed with Accuracy.

## Arkansas Traveler

FOLK SONG

## Melody From The Opera 'Carmen'

BIZET

## Durang's Hornpipe